COMMANDING HER FUTURE

RECLAIMING LEADERSHIP, REST AND LEGACY IN THE AGE OF AI

Rochelle Byrd

Commanding Her Future

Copyright © 2025 by Rochelle Byrd
All rights reserved.

No part of this publication may be reproduced, stored in a retrieval system, distributed or transmitted in any form or by any means electronic, mechanical, photocopying, recording, or otherwise without prior written permission of the publisher, except in the case of brief quotations embodied in critical articles or reviews.

For permissions or inquiries, contact:
- Book@RochelleByrd.com
- www.RochelleByrd.com

ISBN: 979-8-9933399-0-0

Printed in the United States of America.
First Edition, 10/2025
Cover design Rochelle Byrd
Interior design and layout by Rochelle Byrd

Dedication

This book was not written alone.

To my family: your patience, love, and belief gave me the space to create.

To my mentors: thank you for modeling what leadership with integrity looks like.

To every woman who trusted me with her story your vulnerability became the blueprint for this book.

To the AspiraHer community: thank you for reminding me that purpose is scalable.

To my fellow veterans: your courage continues to inspire me beyond the uniform.

And finally, to every woman reading this thank you for choosing to lead differently.

Index

Preface	1
Introduction	2
CHAPTER 1 From Orders to Ownership	4
CHAPTER 2 Burnout & the Broken Ladder	10
CHAPTER 3 What They Never Told Us About AI	17
CHAPTER 4 The R.E.A.L. AI Leadership Framework™	24
CHAPTER 5 Tech Without Purpose Is Just Noise	32
CHAPTER 6 Building a Digital Empire as a Busy Woman	39
CHAPTER 7 The New Table	46
CHAPTER 8 Your 21-Day Activation Plan	53
Glossary	66
Appendix: AI Tools & How I Use Them	67
References & Inspiration	68
Final Command	69

Preface

I didn't set out to write a book.

I set out to find my way through transition, through motherhood, through burnout, through leadership models that never quite fit.

This book was born from questions:

- What if I didn't have to hustle to be worthy?
- What if leadership could include softness, rest, and strategy?
- What if AI wasn't just a tech trend but a tool to help women reclaim time, voice, and legacy?

I'm not a tech genius. I'm not a traditional CEO.
I'm a woman who's been in the trenches military, marriage, motherhood, ministry, and mindset.
And this book is for any woman who's ever asked,
"What now?" and been bold enough to answer with,
"Something better."

This is your invitation to build *your* table.
Your movement. Your legacy.
With systems, sisterhood, and strategy that honors your whole self.

Let's get to work.
Rochelle Byrd

Introduction

There comes a moment when you stop waiting for someone to hand you permission and you realize the mission is yours to lead.

For me, that moment didn't come on a battlefield or in a boardroom. It came at a kitchen table, with a toddler on my hip, a laptop on the counter, and a burning question in my soul: *What now?*

I'd done the military career served over 23 years leading, mentoring, and managing logistics and people across high stakes environments. I'd survived Hurricane Katrina, rebuilt my life from scratch, raised babies while building businesses, earned degrees while navigating divorce, love, loss, and leadership in a system not built for women like me. And yet, here I was… still evolving.

Then came the whisper:

What if leadership wasn't about working harder, but leading smarter?

That's when I met my next soldier in the fight: **AI.**

Artificial Intelligence didn't replace my grind. It amplified my gifts. It gave me back time, clarity, and creativity. It helped me reimagine what leadership could look like for me, for other women veterans, for wives and moms, for

CEOs, for the woman reading this right now... wondering if it's too late to start again.

This book is not about coding or becoming a tech guru.
It's about **owning your voice**, activating your potential, and building something real using tools that are already at your fingertips.
I'm not a tech expert.
I'm a mother. A wife. A nonprofit CEO. A doctoral student.
And I'm *commanding my future* with AI by my side.

So let's get started. It's your turn now.

CHAPTER 1

From Orders to Ownership

Shifting from structure to sovereignty, from survival to strategy.

In the Army, structure isn't optional, it's survival.
You learn to follow before you lead.
To execute before you question.
To stand in formation, even when your spirit wants to run wild.

That kind of discipline?
It shaped me. It served me. It saved me.

But once I stepped out of uniform, into motherhood, entrepreneurship, and community service

I was hit with a painful truth:

Following orders won't build the life you truly want. Ownership will.

✷ The Hidden Cost of Command

We were trained to execute someone else's vision.
To climb ladders built by systems that weren't designed for women like us.

To suppress, conform, survive and then say thank you for the opportunity.

Let me keep it all the way real:
I did all of it.

- ☑ I overachieved.
- ☑ I overcommitted.
- ☑ I overextended.

I became the woman everyone could count on but the one who couldn't always count on herself.

Until one day, I stopped asking for permission.
I stopped waiting for a seat at the table.

I built the damn table.

And that's when the shift happened.
I stopped living like I was in someone else's chain of command and started acting like the **CEO of my life**.

From Chain of Command ↠ Chain of Impact

Let's redefine what leadership means in this new chapter of your life.

Ownership doesn't mean you have all the answers.
It means you're willing to take responsibility for your next move, even if it scares you.

I started asking myself questions that the military never trained me to ask:

- What legacy am I really building?
- What kind of life am I modeling for my children?
- What tools am I using to lead in this modern, messy, magical world?
- What am I tolerating that's keeping me in survival mode instead of walking in strategy mode?

Those questions changed everything.

💡 Real Talk for Women Leaders

If you've ever:

- Felt like you were *leading from the sidelines*
- Been the *only woman or woman of color in the room*
- Struggled to *balance ambition with your mental health*
- Wondered how to *turn your story into something scalable, profitable, and meaningful*

Then sis, you're not alone.
I wrote this book for us.

Because **ownership starts with awareness**.

And awareness demands we stop pretending that old leadership models work.
They don't.

They were never built with us in mind.

But now?
We've got tools.
We've got tech.
We've got each other.
We've got **AI**. **Authenticity**. And **audacity**.

Soldier to CEO: The Mindset Shift

Let's break it down.

Military Mindset	AI-Empowered Leadership
Follow orders	Create systems
Execute tasks	Build strategies
Wait for promotion	Design your path
Lead by title	Lead by value
Suppress emotion	Leverage empathy
Accept burnout	Enforce boundaries

Ownership means you stop waiting for the world to tell you who you are.
You decide.

And then you build the business, brand, legacy and life to match.

🗣 Your Turn: Activate the Shift

Start small.

Pick one area of your life that you've been outsourcing your **schedule**, your **story**, your **strategy** and decide today:

🔑 "I'm reclaiming that."

Because ownership isn't just a mindset.
It's a mission.

And you?

You're built for it.

Affirmation of the Chapter:

"I no longer wait for permission. I lead with power, purpose, and alignment. I am the CEO of my future."

Journal Prompt:

Where in my life have I been following someone else's blueprint instead of designing my own?

_____

_____

_____

_____

Action Step:

Choose *one* decision today that reflects ownership not obligation.

- Say no without guilt
- Speak up in that meeting
- Block out your CEO hours
- Automate one draining task
- Write a new vision for this next season

Small decisions build empires.

Refinement Summary:

- **Voice preserved** strong, inspiring, direct, unapologetic
- **Cadence improved** clear sections with breathing room

- **Clarity enhanced** no fluff, no repetition, just power
- **Call to action** elevated stronger emotional close

CHAPTER 2
Burnout & the Broken Ladder

Reclaiming your energy, redefining success, and disrupting the myth of the "strong woman" who must suffer in silence.

The Unseen Exhaustion

Let me ask you something real...

Have you ever been praised for your strength while silently drowning in exhaustion?

Told you were "doing it all" when deep down, you didn't want to do **any of it like this anymore?**

That, my sister, is **burnout dressed as bravery.**
And we've been conditioned to wear it like a badge of honor.

The Culture of Overload

In the military, you push through.
In corporate, you prove yourself.
In motherhood, you pour out.
In service, you sacrifice.

And in all of it
you smile through the pain,
because the world told you:
"Strong women don't quit."

But let me be completely honest with you:
Strong women break.

Not in boardrooms.
Not in headlines.
But in bathrooms.
In locked cars.
In midnight moments when no one is watching.

We don't quit, but we do disappear.

We disappear from our joy.
We disappear from our passions.
We disappear from the dreams we once carried
before life layered us with **responsibility and survival mode.**

That's burnout.

🔔 Burnout Sounds Like…

If you've ever said:

"I'm just tired all the time."
"There's never enough hours in the day."
"No one really sees how much I do."

…then this chapter is *for you*.

Burnout isn't just exhaustion.
It's **soul depletion**.
It's functioning on autopilot while your spirit waves a white flag.

🪜 The Broken Ladder

Let's talk about this so-called "ladder to success."

You know the one.

We were told:
Get the degrees.
Follow the rules.
Wait your turn.
Work twice as hard to get half as far.

If we were lucky?
We might retire with a pension, a plaque, and a piece of ourselves missing.

But here's the truth nobody told us:
The ladder was never designed for women like us.

Especially not for women who lead with empathy.
Not for women juggling babies and businesses.
Not for women whose greatness makes the room uncomfortable.

Even when we climb it ~ it rarely leads to freedom.

🧱 Why the Ladder is Broken:

It's rigid ~ doesn't bend for babies.
It's shallow ~ no space for healing.
It's biased ~ doesn't reward emotional intelligence.
It's exhausting ~ success comes wrapped in sacrifice.

The ladder demands everything and gives back status with strings attached.

That's not leadership.
That's **performance**.

And we've been performing long enough.

💥 From Burnout to Boldness

My turning point didn't come in a keynote or a boardroom.

It came in my bathroom
whispering into the mirror:

"I don't want to do this anymore."

Not because I couldn't.
But because I realized I didn't want to **keep surviving leadership** that wasn't built for me.

So I made a decision:

"I will no longer burn out trying to fit into systems I was called to transform."

That's when I discovered a *new kind of ally*:
Artificial Intelligence.

🤖 AI = The Liberation Tool You Didn't Know You Needed

Now don't get it twisted:
AI didn't cure my burnout.

But it did give me something I hadn't had in years.

Space.

- Space to think.
- Space to breathe.
- Space to dream again.

AI helped me:

Automate manual tasks
Schedule content in minutes

Plan events, launches, and campaigns without losing sleep
Write emails, proposals, and presentations faster

It didn't make me superhuman ~ it helped me feel human *again*.

Because when you're running a household, leading a team, healing trauma, and trying to walk in purpose?

You don't need more pressure.
You need **permission to do it differently**.

AI gave me that.

 Let's Redefine Strength

Real strength isn't found in burnout.
It's found in **boundaries**.

It's not in doing it all ~ it's in building systems that support it all.

You deserve:

- ✦ Rest without guilt
- ✦ Visibility without performance
- ✦ Impact without burnout
- ✦ Leadership without self-abandonment

And yes, you can still be:

A boss
A mama
A wife
A CEO
A Soldier

A speaker
...while using tech to help you breathe.

That's the shift.

🛠 Burnout Breakthrough Exercise

📝 Journal Prompt:

Where in my life am I still working like a machine, when I could be leading like a women?

_____
_____
_____
_____

✅ Quick Wins:

Try one this week:

- ⏱ Identify one task to automate (email, content, scheduling, admin)
- 💬 Use ChatGPT to draft something you've been procrastinating
- 🛌 Block 2 hours of *non-negotiable* rest ~ not Netflix, but soul-restoring refueling

👑 Affirmation:

"I am no longer available for burnout.
I lead from a place of wholeness ~ not hustle."

🔖 Chapter Close:

Burnout isn't proof of your greatness.

It's a warning sign that you've been too strong, for too long, with too little support.

Let this be your turning point.

Let this be the chapter where you stop surviving ~ and start leading with strategy, rest, and systems.

Because queen...
You were not made to collapse under pressure.

You were made to **rebuild the system**.

Let us keep going.

CHAPTER 3

What They Never Told Us About AI

AI is not the enemy ~ it is the equalizer. But no one told us that.

Rewriting the Narrative

When most people hear "AI," their minds go straight to:

Robots
Job loss
Sci-fi disasters
Tech bros in Silicon Valley

That is not our story.

Because what they never told us ~ especially as women, Black women, veterans, mothers, and mission-driven leaders ~ is this:

AI is not the enemy. It is the equalizer.

But they did not want us to know that.
Because once we understand what AI *actually* does?
We stop settling for scraps ~ and start building empires.

🧠 AI Is not Here to Replace You ~ It is Here to Reclaim You

Let us get something clear.

AI will not do your laundry.
It will not raise your babies.
It will not heal your heartbreak.

But what it *will* do is give you something far more valuable:
Your time, your clarity, your creativity.

When I met AI, I was not a tech expert.
I was not coding or building apps.

I was a **tired woman.**

A woman with:

Too many tabs open, in life and in her brain
Too many ideas stuck on sticky notes
Too many roles, with too little support

I did not need a robot.
I needed *relief.*

So I opened ChatGPT and typed my first prompt:

"Help me write a speech on burnout for women leaders."

What it gave me was not perfect ~ but it was a *spark.*
A reminder that I did not have to do everything alone.

I am the brain. AI is the assistant.

🔧 How I Started Using AI (Without Losing My Mind)

I started small.

With ChatGPT, I began to:

Draft emails that used to take me 30 minutes
Write proposals and course outlines in minutes

Brainstorm social captions and client messaging
Organize launch timelines and event agendas

Then I explored **Canva AI**:
Designed event flyers in under ten minutes
Created branding kits, pitch decks, and reels
Wrote social media captions and lead magnets

Then came **Notion AI, Zapier, Stripe integrations,** and more.

Before I knew it, I was unlocking new levels like it was digital bootcamp.
And the more I leaned in, the more I realized:

This is not about tech. This is about strategy. This is about freedom.

● Let Us Debunk the Lies

Let us clear up some of the biggest lies keeping women out of the AI conversation:

✖ **Lie #1: "AI is too complicated for someone like me."**
☑ Truth: If you can send an email or post on Instagram, you can use AI.

✖ **Lie #2: "AI is going to replace human jobs."**
☑ Truth: AI replaces **repetitive tasks**, not purpose-driven leadership.

It supports humans who lead with heart, strategy, and vision.

✖ **Lie #3: "Only tech experts use AI tools."**
☑ Truth: Most modern AI tools are designed for **creatives**, **coaches**, **educators**, **entrepreneurs**, and **women like YOU** ~ no coding required.

💥 The Moment It Clicked for Me

I was prepping a keynote, exhausted, eyes glazed over staring at a blank Google Doc.
My youngest was finally asleep.
My husband was getting some rest.
And I still had a deadline to meet.

So I typed into ChatGPT:
"Give me 3 stories I could use to open a keynote on burnout and women in leadership."

And just like that ~ I was not starting from scratch.
I had a foundation.
I had a direction.
I had *breathing room*.

Since that night, I have used AI to:
Launch product lines
Create nonprofit strategies
Plan speaking events
Build digital workbooks
Map out my book (yes, this one!)
Automate family schedules
Design revenue models in hours, not months

And I did it all while being fully present for my family.

🔁 The Leadership Shift

In old leadership models, the **loudest voice** wins.
In AI-powered leadership, the **clearest vision** wins.

That is the shift.

AI does not give you your purpose — it **amplifies** it.

It does not make you a leader ~ it makes your leadership **undeniable**.

🎯 Beginner AI Tools I Recommend

Do not try to master everything at once.

Start with one tool. Make it yours.

Tool	Use Case	Ease of Use
ChatGPT	Writing, planning, content ideas	★★★★☆
Canva AI	Design, captions, visual branding	★★★★★
Notion AI	Organizing, content planning	★★★★☆
Trello AI	Task & time management	★★★★☆
Descript	Video editing + captions	★★★★★

🎯 **Pro Tip:** Start by giving one of these tools *one job* ~ not your whole life.

🗣️ Real Talk: AI Will not Save You ~ But It Will Support You

Let us be clear.

AI is not here to "save" your life.
It is here to help you rebuild it with intention.

It is a system ~ not a savior.
A co-pilot ~ not the captain.

Use AI to:

Multiply your message
Streamline your workflow
Reclaim your peace
Reinforce your boundaries
Reduce the mental load that is keeping you stuck

You do not need to hustle harder.
You just need **better systems**.

🛠 AI Activation Exercise

☑ Prompt Challenge:

Open ChatGPT and try one of these today:

"Write a 3-day content plan for a women's empowerment group focused on golf and leadership."

"Give me 5 subject lines for a nonprofit email campaign promoting an event."

"Help me outline a 4-week training program for women veterans transitioning into entrepreneurship."

Just try it. No pressure. No perfection.
Play until the fear fades and the clarity flows.

_____
_____
_____
_____
_____
_____
_____
_____
_____
_____

_____
_____
_____
_____
_____
_____
_____

💭 Mindset Shift:

"I am not behind. I am not late.
I am right on time ~ and AI is my accelerator, not my replacement."

👑 Affirmation of the Chapter:

"I lead with purpose. I build with systems.
I reclaim my time, my creativity, and my legacy ~ with AI by my side."

They did not build AI with women like us in mind.
But guess what?

We are using it anyway ~ **and we're building something better**.

This chapter isn't about tech.
It's about *transformation*.

Now that you see what's possible?

Let's talk about how to lead *with purpose* ~ not pressure ~ using the framework that changed everything for me.

CHAPTER 4

The R.E.A.L. AI Leadership Framework™

Leadership is no longer about hustle and hierarchy ~ it's about clarity, authenticity, systems, and scaling with ease. R.E.A.L. gives women a new model to build and lead in alignment.

Let's Be R.E.A.L.

Leadership in 2025?
It doesn't look like it did in 1995.

We don't have time for:

Ego-driven titles
Outdated playbooks
Work cultures that glorify burnout and ignore brilliance

The world has changed.
We've changed.

And now?
It's time for a leadership framework that honors that change.

Women ~ especially women veterans, mothers, and mission-driven professionals ~ are done with the status quo.

We don't just want to lead.

We want to **lead well**.
And we want to do it with clarity, confidence, and systems that *protect our peace*.

🔑 The Truth About Leadership + AI

Let's be honest:

AI without purpose is just noise.
And leadership without authenticity?
That's just performance.

We need both:

- *Systems* that work behind the scenes
- *Values* that anchor everything we build
- *Vision* that scales without self-abandonment

So I created a new blueprint:

🎯 The R.E.A.L. AI Leadership Framework™

A system to help you lead with intention, scale with ease, and show up as the *real you* in every room, on every platform, in every mission.

Letter	Pillar	Purpose
R	Reimagine	Shift your mindset. Redefine leadership on *your* terms.
E	Equip	Learn the tools. Use AI to automate, organize, and scale.
A	Amplify	Expand your voice, visibility, and reach.
L	Lead Authentically	Build in alignment with who you are ~ not who they told you to be.

📌 Why This Framework Works:

It's not tech-heavy
It's built for real life ~ not theory

You don't need perfection ~ just commitment

It meets you where you are ~ and helps you build where you're going

This isn't another course.
This isn't another 40-hour certification.
This is a *code to lead your life by*.

✨ R: Reimagine

Before you build anything, you've got to believe it's possible.

Reimagining leadership means:

Dismantling old definitions
Releasing titles that no longer serve you
Refusing to play small for comfort

You don't need to:

Sound like a man
Outwork your trauma
Earn another degree
Get a million followers

You just need a clear vision ~ and the courage to lead like *you*.

💭 Ask Yourself:

What does *ease* look like in my leadership?
What would success feel like without burnout?

Who told me leadership had to look one way?
AI won't fix a broken vision ~ but it will **magnify a clear one**.

💼 E: Equip

Here's where it gets fun.

Equipping yourself doesn't mean becoming a tech genius. It means becoming a *systems builder*.

If you're still doing everything manually?
Sis, you're already behind.

Let's change that.

Equip Yourself With:

ChatGPT: Ideas, content, emails, planning
Canva AI: Visuals, branding, social posts
Notion AI: Business planning, weekly dashboards
Trello or ClickUp: Task + team management
Zapier: Back-end automations
Descript: Podcast and video editing

Start with **ONE tool**.

Master it.
Make it serve *you*.
Then build from there.

Systems don't steal your power.
They give it structure.

🎤 A: Amplify

This is where we get LOUD.

Once you've reimagined your vision and equipped your systems ~
It's time to amplify your voice.

Your story is not too much.

Your message is not too niche.
Your voice is not too late.

Use AI to Amplify By:

Turning one video into 10 reels, captions, and blogs
Repurposing stories across platforms (ChatGPT + Descript = magic)
Turning your message into a book, podcast, product, or course
Launching an offer with a funnel you build in an afternoon

You're not just building a brand.
You're building a movement.

And movements need volume.

Let AI help you multiply your magic.

🔸 L: Lead Authentically

This is the anchor of the framework.
Because what is the point of building something ~ if you lose yourself in the process?

Let us get something straight:

AI does not define you.
You define how you use it.

You do not have to:

Sound like anybody else
Market like anybody else

Mimic masculine leadership.
Abandon your softness to be seen as strong.

Real Leadership = Aligned Leadership

Lead with:

Empathy
Integrity
Boundaries

Systems that support your brilliance

Your leadership doesn't have to be loud to be legendary. It has to be **true**.

AI should help you protect your peace ~ not pollute it.

🧠 Ask Yourself:

What makes me magnetic as a leader?
What legacy am I building?
How can I lead without abandoning the woman I'm becoming?

🧠 A Final Word on the R.E.A.L. Method

You do not need to do it all at once.
You do not need a perfect 5-year plan.
You need one bold decision:

"I'm ready to lead differently."

And once you decide that?
Everything else starts falling into place.

You do not have to build alone.
You have support ~ in community, in tools, and inside yourself.

Let us activate this framework and start building something sustainable.

🛠 Your R.E.A.L. Activation Plan

💬 Journal Prompt:

Which pillar do I feel most confident in?
Which one am I avoiding ~ and why?

_____
_____
_____
_____
_____

✅ Action Step:

Pick **ONE** pillar this week.

Examples:

R = Rewrite your leadership vision
E = Choose a new tool and try it
A = Post your message online
L = Set a boundary that honors your energy

👑 Affirmation:

"I lead with vision.
I scale with wisdom.
I walk in alignment ~ and I do it all while being R.E.A.L."

This is not just a framework.
It is a philosophy.
It is a life strategy.
It is a future-focused operating system for women who are done surviving ~ and ready to *lead*.

Now that you have got the blueprint...

Let's talk about what happens when we use tools without **alignment**.

CHAPTER 5

Tech Without Purpose Is Just Noise

Let Us Cut Through the Fluff

You do not need another app.
You do not need another tab open.
You do not need another "must-have tool" in your inbox.

What you really need is:

- ✨ **Clarity**
- ✨ **Alignment**
- ✨ **Purpose**

Because here is the truth:

Automation without alignment is just noise.

And in this season of your life?
You do not have time for noise.

🦉 The Digital Hustle is Real

AI is everywhere.
Every day there is a new platform, plugin, tool, or shortcut promising to "change your life."

So you:

Download the free trial.
Test the new app.
Add another tool to your tech stack.
Tell yourself it is "productive"!

But let us be honest.
What actually happens?

That tool collects dust.
Your to-do list stays long.
And your mental load grows heavier.

That is not digital strategy.
That is **digital hustle**.

And sis ~ hustle by any other name is still burnout.

🔄 Why We Get Caught Up in the Tech Trap

Let us be real:

We want relief, not more responsibility.
We want shortcuts, not stress.

We are looking for *systems* ~ not more steps.
But too often, we confuse **doing more** with **doing what matters**.

💡 Purpose Before Platform

Before you download one more tool, ask yourself:

What do I actually need this tool to do?

Will this buy me back time ~ or steal more of it?

Is this aligned with my long-term vision ~ or just another distraction?

Because here is the shift:

Old Model	New Model
Use all the tools	Use what serves your mission
Jump on every trend	Focus on your system
Build around tech	Build around *purpose*

Do not build your business around a platform. Build it around your *purpose* ~ and let tech support it.

🛠 Tools Are Not Strategy

Let me say this loud for the high-achievers in the back:

Tools are not strategy.

Tools follow strategy.

You do not need:

ChatGPT Pro to start writing.
Canva Premium to post content.
A full funnel to serve your people.

You need:

Clarity
Consistency
Courage to begin.

Case in Point:

When I launched **AspiraHer**, I did not start with a website or an automation funnel.

I started with a *mission*:

To create spaces where women could feel bold, well, and seen.

Then I asked:

How can tech help me do this *faster*?
How can automation give me more space to *serve*?

And *that is* when the systems came.

So, remember:

Tech should serve the mission ~ not become the mission.

🔍 Simplify to Scale

Here is one of the biggest lies in modern leadership:

"The more complex your system, the more successful you'll be."

LIES.

Here is what actually scales:

- ☑ Simple systems
- ☑ Repeatable routines
- ☑ Tools you actually use
- ☑ Energy that's *focused*, not frantic

✨ You don't need more tools. You need *more intention*.

🔎 Do a Tech Alignment Audit

Let's get practical.

This week, take 15 minutes to do a **Tech Alignment Audit**. Ask yourself:

Tool / Platform	Do I Use This Weekly?	Does It Save Me Time?	Does It Align with My Goals?
ChatGPT	Yes / No	Yes / No	Yes / No
Canva	Yes / No	Yes / No	Yes / No
Notion / Trello	Yes / No	Yes / No	Yes / No
Zapier	Yes / No	Yes / No	Yes / No
Mailchimp	Yes / No	Yes / No	Yes / No
Others? (List)	Yes / No	Yes / No	Yes / No

If it is not saving time or making your mission easier ~ let it go.

🗣 Real Talk: Don't Let Tech Steal Your Voice

A lot of people use AI to sound "perfect, polished, and professional.
But that is not where the power is.

Your story is the strategy.

Your truth is the traction.

Your tone is the trust.

Do not let AI water that down.

Use tech to:

Clarify your message
Organize your brilliance
Build consistency

But don't let it erase the **YOU** in your brand.

People don't connect with perfection. They connect with presence.

So show up, even when it's messy.
Be loud, even when it's not polished.
Be *real*, even when you're using AI.

☑ Alignment Checklist

Use this checklist anytime you feel overwhelmed or distracted by tech:

✓ Does this task need to be **automated** ~ or eliminated entirely?

✓ Am I using tech as a **tool**, not a crutch?
✓ Does this system reflect how I want to **feel** ~ not just what I want to *do*?

✦ Use AI to protect your time ~ not to overcommit it.

⚒ Alignment Exercise

💬 Journal Prompt:

Where in my life am I confusing productivity with purpose?

_____

_____

_____

_____

☑ Action Step:

Audit your top 3 tech tools.

Let go of the one that no longer serves your vision.

Replace "doing more" with "doing what matters."

👑 Affirmation:

"I do not chase trends.
I build strategy.

I do not use tech to be busy ~ I use it to stay aligned with the woman I'm becoming."

Let us be clear:

You do not need more pressure.

You do not need more noise.

You need:

A mission that moves you
A system that supports you
And the wisdom to say "no" to what no longer fits

This is not about having the fanciest tools.
It's about having **the courage to lead with clarity.**

Let's build your digital empire with that in mind.

CHAPTER 6
Building a Digital Empire as a Busy Woman

Let's Keep it 💯

You are not just:

A mom
A wife
A veteran
A student
A leader

You are an **empire builder** in motion.

You have got:

Legacy on your back
Vision in your mind
Purpose in your soul
And still...

Some days you cannot find your phone.
The toddler's eating crayons.
Your DMs are a mess.
And your inbox says *1,202 unread*.

Sound familiar?

This is not fantasy leadership.
This is **real-life leadership** ~ and it is messy, magical, and mission-driven.

✳ The Empire Code

Here is the truth:

You do not need **more time** ~ you need a system.
You do not need to **do it all** ~ you need automation.
You do not need to **shrink** ~ you need strategy.

Let me show you how I:

Run three brands
Lead a nonprofit
Raise my family
Coach clients
Speak on stages

And still **pour back into myself**

Spoiler alert: It is not perfect.

But it is **purposeful**.
And that is what makes it *sustainable*.

👩‍💼 Empire Snapshot: What is on My Plate

I do not share this to impress you ~ I share it to show you what's *possible*.

💼 My Businesses:

AspiraHer Inc. – A nonprofit women's empowerment brand blending golf, wellness, and leadership

Body Burn Athletics – A fitness and apparel brand for bold, busy women

Saintsational Flavors – A New Orleans-inspired catering and digital food brand

D & D Transportation Express – A Logistics Company.

🧠 My Roles:

Doctoral student

Army HR & Logistics Officer (retirement on the horizon!)

Wife, mama of 4

Coach, speaker, and course creator

⚙️ My Digital Toolbox:

These are my go-to tools — *not to look fancy*, but to stay focused and free.

Tool	Purpose
ChatGPT	Brainstorming, content writing, automation scripts
Canva	Graphics, flyers, social media, lead magnets
Notion	Weekly planning, content calendars, brand strategy
Stripe	Automated payments, coaching programs
Zapier	System integration (so I don't do it all manually)
Mailchimp	Email newsletters + event announcements
Shopify / Stan Store	Digital product sales & storefronts
Google Workspace	Docs, spreadsheets, contracts, files

I don't use all of these every single day.
But they each hold a piece of the empire.

🎙️ My AI-Powered Daily Rhythm

🌅 Morning: Set the Vibe, Not the Vibe Check

🎤 Voice-note my to-do list → Plug it into Notion

💬 ChatGPT prompt: "Write a caption about rest and alignment"
🎨 Canva: Design a matching graphic in under 5 minutes
📅 Schedule via Buffer or Meta Planner

By 8 AM, I've shown up for my brand ~ without burning out my brain.

🕛 Midday: Mini CEO Hour

(Usually during nap time, lunch, or post-gym)

✅ Check Stripe: "You received a payment" 💰
✅ Respond to speaking inquiries with ChatGPT-generated replies
✅ Review coaching calls or nonprofit tasks
✅ Knock out 1–2 high-priority items from my Notion dashboard

I don't grind. I flow. And systems make that possible.

🌙 Evening: Reset & Reflect

🧘 Reflect: "What worked today? What felt heavy?"
✅ Update Trello board — move completed tasks
💬 Use ChatGPT: "Summarize this client call for notes"
📧 Schedule emails or reminders for the next day

Then I **shut it down** — because rest *is* strategy.

💰 Income Without Burnout

Here's what most people don't tell you:

You don't build a digital empire by *doing everything yourself.*

You build it by designing **systems that work when you don't.**

🔸 My Automated Income Flow:

Brand	Revenue Source	AI & Automation Assist
AspiraHer	Event tickets, grants, merch	Canva flyers, ChatGPT emails, Eventbrite templates
Body Burn	Apparel + supplements	Shopify automations, email campaigns
Saintsational	Digital recipes, cooking demos	ChatGPT formatting, Canva eBook design
Speaking / Coaching	1:1 clients, masterclasses	Stripe + Notion CRM + automated lead flows

You don't need 100K followers.

You need:
A **clear offer**
A **repeatable system**
And the **right tools** to scale your brilliance

🔸 What I Had to Let Go to Grow

Here's what I had to **release** in order to rise:

✖ Perfectionism
✖ Doing everything solo
✖ Saying "yes" out of guilt
✖ Systems I couldn't sustain
✖ Leadership models that ignored my *wholeness*

I stopped trying to "keep up."
I started designing a life I didn't need to escape from.

AI gave me more than tools.
It gave me *permission* to stop doing it the hard way.

Empire Building Exercise

💬 Journal Prompt:

What parts of my day could be automated, delegated, or eliminated entirely?

_____

_____

_____

_____

✅ Quick Action:

Write down 3 tasks that drain your time **daily**.

Now ask.

Can I automate this?
Can I delegate this?
Can I eliminate this?

Need help? Literally ask ChatGPT:

"What tools can automate [insert task] for a busy woman entrepreneur?"

👑 Affirmation:

"I am the CEO of my life.

I build with clarity.
I rest with confidence.
I lead from overflow ~ not burnout."

You don't have to choose between impact and rest.

You don't have to do it all ~you just have to **design systems that do what you no longer need to carry.**

Your digital empire doesn't have to look like anyone else's.
It doesn't have to be loud or perfect.
It just has to be *real*, *aligned*, and *yours*.

In the next chapter, we're going beyond systems ~
and straight into **legacy**.

Because there comes a time when you stop asking for a seat...
and start building the table.

CHAPTER 7

The New Table

The Shift

There comes a moment when you stop asking for a seat at the table...

Not because you've given up ~
But because you've outgrown *waiting to be included*.

You don't need a longer table.
You don't need a louder voice.
You don't need a more comfortable corner in someone else's structure.

You need something *new*.

So you build it.

Not just a seat.
Not just a room.
But a **new table** ~ one rooted in clarity, equity, healing, and legacy.

And let me be clear:

We are not waiting to be invited into the future.
We are leading it.

🛡 Why the Old Table Doesn't Work

The traditional leadership tables ~ in corporate, military, tech, politics, and even nonprofits ~ weren't built for:

Our rhythm

Our voices
Our lived experiences
Our leadership style

They reward:

Hustle
Hyper-productivity
Ego-driven performance

They punish:

Empathy
Vulnerability
Slowness
Rest

These tables ask women ~ especially **Black and Brown women** ~ to:

Code-switch
Play small
Shrink brilliance

Say "thank you" just for being in the room

Nah.
That's not leadership ~ that's survival.

And we?
We're **done surviving systems** that gaslight our greatness.

🛠 What the New Table Looks Like

So I built a new table.
And at this table, we live by *different rules.*

At this table:

Rest is a leadership strategy
Ease is not a weakness ~ it's a system
Purpose pays
Joy is non-negotiable
Automation is self-care
Boundaries are sacred
We speak in our full voice ~ without apology

This table is:

Digitally powered
Women-centered
Future-forward
Faith-aligned
Community-backed
Rooted in *vision over validation*

We don't just bring resumes.
We bring *receipts* ~ of resilience, innovation, and soul work.

🌍 Who Sits at This Table?

This table is not exclusive ~ it's *intentional*.

It's for:

The woman veteran transitioning from service to CEO
The HR professional tired of knowing more than her director
The nonprofit founder doing $100K of labor on a $0 salary
The mama building a business during nap time
The thought leader finally ready to lead in her own name
The woman who's done waiting ~ and ready to *build*

And most of all?

It's for **you** ~ the woman reading this who knows she's *meant for more.*

🤖 This Table Has WiFi and Purpose

Yes, we use AI.
Yes, we love tools.

But they don't lead us ~ **we do**.

At this table:

We automate what drains us
We delegate what distracts us
We align our tech with our truth
We protect our energy like an asset ~ because it is

AI is the assistant.
You are the architect.

This isn't about building a personal brand that looks good on Instagram.
It's about building a **life** that aligns with your spirit, your mission, and your future.

📣 Reclaiming Your Leadership Identity

Let's make something clear:

You don't need to:

Get another certification
Wait until you're "polished"
Hit 10K followers
Be less opinionated
Shrink to be digestible

You are not just ready.
You are called.

Leadership isn't about checking boxes anymore.
It's about *choosing yourself* ~ and building structures that reflect your values.

You're not just part of the conversation.
You are the conversation.

You're not just joining rooms.
You're designing them.

You are not just "next."
You are *now*.

💬 Empire-Building from the Inside Out

Here's the truth:

You don't build the new table through hustle.

You build it with:

- 💡 Vision
- 🛠 Systems
- 💝 Sisterhood
- 🧘 Boundaries
- 🧠 AI-powered support
- 🙏 And a whole lot of faith

You do not have to explain yourself.
You do not have to beg.

You just **build**.
And when you build boldly ~
You attract the women who were always meant to sit beside you.

The New Table Exercise

💬 Journal Prompt:

If I built my own leadership table, what would it look like?

Who's there?
What values are honored?
What's being served?
What are the non-negotiables?

_____
_____
_____
_____

✅ Action Step:

Write a "**New Table" vision statement.**

It could sound like this:

"I'm building a leadership space where rest is sacred, voices are valued, systems are soul-aligned, and women rise without apology."

Then post it:

On your mirror
On your phone wallpaper
On your IG story
Inside your team Slack
In your group chat

Say it out loud.
Speak it into your systems.

Let the world know ~ this is not a trend.

This is **a table.**
And it's yours.

♛ Affirmation:

"I am not waiting for a seat.
I am building the table.

I lead with boldness, vision, and joy ~
and I bring other women with me."

This is bigger than strategy.
It is **a shift in sovereignty.**

You're not just leading a business.
You're building a new model of leadership ~ rooted in rest, equity, automation, and truth.

And now?

It's time to **activate** everything you have learned.

Because a blueprint means nothing without movement.

CHAPTER 8

Your 21-Day Activation Plan

Sis, It is Time to Move

You have read.
You have reflected.
You have reimagined, equipped, amplified, and led.

But let me be clear:

Nothing changes if nothing activates.

The difference between dreaming and building?

- ☑ Action.
- ☑ Intention.
- ☑ Consistency.

That's why I created this 21-Day Activation Plan ~ not to add more pressure, but to help you build *momentum* in small, powerful steps.

This is not about hustle.
This is about alignment.
This is your launch pad.

Let's get to work.

How to Use This Plan

Do one prompt or action per day
Each day builds on the one before it

Do not skip ~ but if you fall behind, just *pick up where you left off*

Journal it. Voice-note it. Speak it out loud. Whatever works for you

Need support? Use ChatGPT to co-create along the way

✦ You do not need perfection.
You need *activation*.

🚀 Week 1: Reimagine Your Vision

This week is about *resetting your mindset* and expanding what is possible.

☑ Day 1 – Declare It

Prompt:

What am I really building? What is the big, bold vision?

💬 Example:

"I am building a digital brand that empowers women veterans to use AI to reclaim their time and voice."

_____

_____

_____

_____

☑ Day 2 – Release It

Prompt:

What do I need to let go of to grow?
(Fear, perfection, old labels, shame, grind culture)

_____

_____

☑ Day 3 – Rewrite the Rules

Prompt:

What leadership rules no longer serve me?

💬 Example:

"Rest is not weakness. Delegation is strength."

_____

_____

_____

_____

☑ Day 4 – Cast the Vision

🔖 **Action:**

Post a public statement of your mission or vision. IG, LinkedIn, email ~ you choose.

Use ChatGPT to help you draft it if you get stuck!

_____

_____

_____

_____

✅ Day 5 – Visualize Your Empire

🎨 **Action:**

Create a digital vision board (Canva, Pinterest, or physical board).

Include:

Brand colors
Power words
AI tools

Your "why" and "who"

_____
_____
_____

✅ Day 6 – Identify Your Zone of Genius

Prompt:

What do people *always* come to me for?
What lights me up when I do it?

_____
_____
_____

✅ Day 7 – Check Your Alignment

Prompt:

Does my current schedule reflect the life I'm building? What needs to shift?

_____
_____
_____
_____

⚙ Week 2: Equip Yourself

Now that your vision is clear, let's build the *systems* to support it.

✅ Day 8 – Audit Your Time

Prompt:

What tasks are draining me daily?
What could be automated or eliminated?

_____
_____
_____
_____

☑ Day 9 – Explore an AI Tool

✶ Action:

Try one:

ChatGPT (content, planning)
Canva AI (design)
Notion AI (systems)
Descript (video editing)

🎯 Don't aim to master it — just play.

_____
_____
_____
_____

☑ Day 10 – Write with AI

✎ Action:

Use ChatGPT to draft something you've been putting off:

A caption
A bio
A brand pitch
A flyer

_____
_____
_____
_____

☑ Day 11 – Create a Content System

📅 Action:

Build a simple 3-day or 7-day content calendar:

Plan posts around your vision
Use templates or AI to generate ideas
Store everything in Trello, Notion, or your phone notes

_____
_____
_____
_____

☑ Day 12 – Build Your AI Toolkit

🛠 Action:

Make a list:

What tools do I already have?
What do I *actually* need?
What's just noise?

Eliminate what doesn't align.

_____
_____
_____
_____

☑ Day 13 – Design a Simple Funnel

◆ Action:

Sketch your customer flow:

Freebie → Email List → Offer
Workshop → DM → Coaching
Event → Product → Follow-up

Keep it messy. Just get it out of your head.

_____
_____
_____
_____

☑ Day 14 – Set Your CEO Hours

🕐 Action:

Block out 2–3 non-negotiable hours/week.

These are your **Empire Hours**.
Protect them like your peace.

_____
_____
_____
_____

🎤 Week 3: Amplify & Lead Authentically

This week is about **visibility**, **impact**, and **real voice leadership**.

☑ Day 15 – Share Your Story

🎙 **Action:**

Post a piece of your story using this framework:

Who I was → What I learned → Who I serve

Can be a post, blog, video, or voice note.

_____
_____
_____
_____

☑ Day 16 – Define Your Offer

Prompt:

What am I actually selling or offering?

💬 Example:

"I help working moms automate their brands using AI and empathy."

_____
_____
_____
_____

☑ Day 17 – Build Your Tribe

👭 Action:

Reach out to 3 women you want to grow with, learn from, or collaborate with.

Affirm them. Tag them. DM them. Don't do this alone.

_____
_____
_____
_____

☑ Day 18 – Speak It Into Existence

🎙 Action:

Record a 1–2 minute video (or voice note) declaring:

What you're building
Why it matters
What's coming next

Save it or post it. Anchor it.

_____
_____
_____
_____

☑ Day 19 – Design Your Empire Map

🗺 Action:

Draw or diagram:

Your brand(s)
Your offers
Your audience
Your revenue streams
Your systems

Visualize how it *all* connects.

_____
_____
_____
_____

☑ Day 20 – Celebrate Yourself

🎉 Prompt:

What have I learned about myself in the past 3 weeks? What shifted in my leadership?

Don't skip this. Integration = Power.

_____
_____
_____
_____

✅ Day 21 – Declare Your Table

📝 Prompt:

"This is the table I'm building.
This is who I'm becoming.
This is how I lead."

Say it. Write it. Post it.
This is your activation declaration.

_____

_____

_____

_____

👑 Final Activation

You've done the inner work.
You've built the outer systems.
Now it's time to **lead out loud**.

Remember:

You are not late.
You are not too much.
You are not behind.
You are **right on time**.

This is not the end of a book.
It's the *beginning of your empire*.

You don't have to hustle like the world told you to.
You just have to lead like the woman you were always meant to be.

Now go.

Lead. Build. Reclaim. Activate.

We're not just commanding our future —
We're *designing* it. 🗽 👑 📓

Glossary

AI (Artificial Intelligence): Computer systems designed to simulate human intelligence tasks like writing, design, and problem solving.

Burnout: A state of emotional, mental, and physical exhaustion caused by prolonged stress, especially in leadership roles.

Automation: The use of technology to complete tasks with little to no human input.

Digital Empire: A system of brands, businesses, and platforms that generate income and impact online.

Zone of Genius: The unique area where your skills, purpose, and joy intersect.

CEO Time / CEO Hours: Dedicated time blocked out to work *on* your business or life, not just in it.

The New Table: A concept and movement rooted in creating leadership spaces that honor the lived experiences, values, and voices of women — especially those historically left out of traditional power structures.

Appendix: AI Tools & How I Use Them

Tool	Function	Pro Tip
ChatGPT	Drafting, brainstorming, automation	Use templates for content, emails, bios
Canva AI	Visual branding, lead magnets, captions	Keep a branded template folder
Notion AI	Planning, systems, client tracking	Create a weekly "CEO Dashboard"
Trello	Task management, project timelines	Assign days to buckets (e.g., Monday: content)
Descript	Video editing, transcript creation	Use for quick podcast or speaking reels
Zapier	Automation between platforms	Start with one Zap: email > folder
Stripe	Client payments, product sales	Automate receipts & contracts with Zapier
Stan Store / Shopify	Selling digital products	Upload eBooks, workbooks, and passive offers

References & Inspiration

While much of this book is based on lived experience, here are a few resources that support the strategies and mindset shifts covered:

- "Burnout: The Secret to Unlocking the Stress Cycle" – Emily Nagoski & Amelia Nagoski

- McKinsey & Company's Women in the Workplace Report (2024)

- Pew Research: The State of Women Leaders in Tech

- Harvard Business Review: Why Empathetic Leadership Matters

- OpenAI & Canva AI documentation

- ChatGPT prompt libraries for entrepreneurs

- Personal conversations, mentorship, and client stories (used with permission)

Final Command

There comes a time when you stop reading leadership books... and start *becoming* the kind of leader they never taught you to be.
If this book planted a seed in you ~ let it grow.
If it confirmed what you already knew ~ let it rise.
If it challenged the way you have been leading ~ let it shift.

This is not the end of the journey.
It is the activation of your next level.

Let me remind you:

You do not need permission.
You do not need perfect timing.
You do not need a fancy title.

You need:

- A clear mission
- A system that protects your peace
- And the courage to lead from *overflow*, not obligation.

You are not just commanding your future.

You are *designing the blueprint* for every woman watching you do it.

I will see you at the table you are building.

With purpose,
Rochelle Byrd

www.ingramcontent.com/pod-product-compliance
Lightning Source LLC
Chambersburg PA
CBHW050918160426
43194CB00011B/2453